quail studio

quail studio

Published in 2017 by
Quail Publishing
The Old Forge,
Market Square,
Toddington
Bedfordshire, LU5 6BP
UK

ISBN: 978-0-9935908-3-2

Conceived, designed and produced by

quail studio

Art Editor: Georgina Brant
Graphic Design: Quail Studio
Technical Editor: Amelia
Photography: Jarek Duk
Yarn Support: Rowan Yarns
Designer: Quail Studio
Model: Eva - BMA Models

Printed in the UK

British Library Cataloguing in Publication Data
A catalogue record for this book is available from the British Library

@quail_studio

contents

introduction

The fourth in the series of ESSENTIAL knits from q u a i l s t u d i o
comes the Accessories collection. Designed by our studio to be
an appealing collection that can be styled in different ways –
completing your essential wardrobe.

The q u a i l s t u d i o team have focussed on bringing texture into a
simple collection, paired with a minimalist colour palette and simple
styling to bring to life the exquisite yarn from Rowan.

Hand knit your own essential stylish accessories to complete your
look. We just know you will not be disappointed!

q u a i l s t u d i o t e a m
xoxo

the patterns

eva
beanie

SIZE: To fit average-size woman's head

YARN USAGE: Rowan Baby Merino Silk DK

A – Zinc 681 x 1 ball
B – Dawn 672 x 2 balls

NEEDLES: 4mm needles (6US)

TENSION: 22sts and 30rows = 10cm measured over stocking stitch using 4mm needles

EXTRAS: Cable needle, pom-pom (optional)

C4B: Slip next 2sts onto cable needle and hold at back of work, knit next 2sts, knit 2sts from cable needle.

Using yarn A and 4mm needles, cast on 116sts.

Row 1: (RS) (K2, P2) to end.
Row 2: (K2, P2) to end.
Rep last 2 rows until work meas 8cm, ending with a WS row. *Change to B*

Next Row: Knit across all sts, increasing 8sts evenly across row. 124sts

Next Row: *K4, P4; rep from * to last 4sts, K4.

Change to yarn B.

Row 1: (RS) *P4, K4; rep from * to last 4sts, P4.
Row 2: *K4, P4; rep from * to last 4sts, K4.
Row 3: As row 1.
Row 4: As row 2.
Row 5: *P4, C4B; rep from * to last 4sts, P4.

Rep rows 2-5 until work meas 28cm, ending after row 5.

Next Row: (WS) *K2tog, K2tog, P4; rep from * to last 4sts, K2tog, K2tog. 92sts
Next Row: *P2, K4; rep from * to last 2sts, P2.
Next Row: *K2tog, P4; rep from * to last 2sts, K2tog. 76sts
Next Row: *P1, K2tog, K2tog; rep from * to last st, P1. 46 sts
Next Row: *K1, P2; rep from * to last st, K1.
Next Row: *P1, K2tog; rep from * to last st, P1. 31sts

FINISHING
Cut yarn, leaving a length long enough to sew up hat.

Pull yarn through rem sts and sew up using mattress stitch, reversing for folded-up section of brim.

Attach pom-pom if desired.

claudia
tassel scarf

YARN USAGE: Rowan Felted Tweed

A – Maritime 167 x 4 balls

B – Alabaster 197 x 5 balls

NEEDLES: 7mm (11US)

TENSION: 16sts and 22 rows = 10cm measured over stocking stitch using 7mm needles and yarn held double

APPROX FINISHED MEASUREMENTS: 240cm x 20cm (excluding tassels)

TASSELS
Cut 256 lengths of yarn B measuring 30cm, group 8 together.

Fold tassels in half, pull folded end front to back through first stitch, pull tail end through folded edge and tighten.

Evenly space 16 tassels each across cast-on and cast-off edges.
32 tassels in total.

Using a strand each of yarn A & B, and 7mm needles, cast on 32sts.

Row 1: Knit.

Row 2: P1, K1, P1, purl to last 3sts, P1, K1, P1.

Rep last 2 rows throughout.
Continue until work meas 240cm ending with a WS row.
Cast off.

clara

snood

YARN USAGE: 3 x 100g balls of Rowan Big Wool (shown in Concrete – 061)

NEEDLES: 10mm needles (15US)

TENSION: 7½sts and 10rows = 10cm measured over moss stitch using 10mm needles

APPROX FINISHED MEASUREMENTS: 30cm x 150cm

FINISHING
Press as described on information page

Using mattress stitch, join cast-on and cast-off edges together.

Using 10mm needles, cast on 22sts.

Row 1: (RS) (K1, P1) to end.
Row 2: (P1, K1) to end.

Rep last 2 rows until work meas 150cm, ending with a WS row.
Cast off.

elle
cable hat

SIZE: To fit average-size adult woman's head

YARN USAGE: 2 x 100g balls of Rowan Cocoon (shown in Dove – 849)

NEEDLES: 6.5mm and 7mm needles (10.5US and 11US)

TENSION: 22sts and 20rows = 10cm measured over cable pattern using 7mm needles

EXTRAS: Cable needle, pom-pom (optional)

C6B: Slip next 3sts onto a cable needle and hold at back of work, knit next 3sts, knit 3sts from cable needle.

C6F: Slip next 3sts onto a cable needle and hold at front of work, knit next 3sts, knit 3sts from cable needle.

Using 6.5mm needles, cast on 80sts.

Row 1: (RS) (K1, P1) to end.
Row 2: (K1, P1) to end.
Rep last 2 rows until work meas 8cm, ending with a WS row.

Change to 7mm needles.
Row 1: (RS) P2, *K12, P1; rep from * to end.
Row 2: *K1, P12; rep from * to last 2sts, K2.
Rep last 2 rows once more.
Row 5: P2, *C6B, C6F, P1; rep from * to end.
Row 6: As row 2.
Row 7: As row 1.
Row 8: As row 2.
Row 9: As row 1.
Row 10: As row 2.
Rep rows 5-10 until hat meas 20cm from rib, ending with a RS row.

Next Row: (WS) *K1, P2, P2tog, P4, P2tog, P2; rep from * to last 2sts, K2. 68sts
Next Row: P2, *K2, K2tog, K2, K2tog, P1; rep from * to end. 56sts
Next Row: *K1, P2, P2tog, P2tog, P2; rep from *to last 2sts, K2. 44sts
Next Row: P2, *K1, K2tog, K2tog, K1, P1; rep from * to end. 32sts

Next Row: *K1, P2tog, P2tog; rep
from * to last 2sts, K2. 20sts
Next Row: K2tog to end. 10sts

FINISHING
Cut yarn, leaving a length long
enough to sew up hat.

Pull yarn through rem sts and sew up
using mattress stitch, reversing for
folded-up section of brim.

Attach pom-pom if desired.

elle

cable snood

YARN USAGE: 2 x 100g balls of Rowan Cocoon (shown in Dove – 849)

NEEDLES: 7mm needles (11US)

TENSION: 14sts and 16rows = 10cm measured over stocking stitch using 7mm needles

EXTRAS: Cable needle

APPROX FINISHED MEASUREMENTS: 75cm x 30cm

Row 1: (RS) P2, K12, P22, K12, P2.
Row 2: K2, P12, K22, P12, K2.
Row 3: P2, C6B, C6F, P22, C6B, C6F, P2.
Row 4: As row 2.
Row 5: As row 1.
Row 6: As row 2.

Rep last 6 rows until work measures 75cm, ending after row 6.

Cast off.

FINISHING

Press as described on the information page.

Holding work wrong sides together, graft seams together.

C6B: Slip next 3sts onto a cable needle and hold at back of work, knit next 3sts, knit 3sts from cable needle.

C6F: Slip next 3sts onto a cable needle and hold at front of work, knit next 3sts, knit 3sts from cable needle.

Using 7mm needles and provisional cast-on method, cast on 50sts.

GRAFTING TECHNIQUE

Holding your two needles side by side, wrong sides facing each other.

Step 1: Insert your needle into the first stitch on the front needle as if to purl. Do not pull the stitch off the needle.

Step 2: Insert your needle into the first stitch on the back needle as if to knit. Do not pull the stitch off the needle.

Step 3: Insert your needle into the first stitch on the front needle as if to knit. Pull this stitch off the needle.

Step 4: Insert your needle into the 'new' first stitch on the front needle as if to purl. Do not pull the stitch off the needle.

Step 5: Insert your needle into the first stitch on the back needle as if to purl. Pull this stitch off the needle.

Step 6: Insert your needle into the 'new' first stitch on the back needle as if to knit. Do not pull the stitch off the needle.

Rep steps 3 – 6 until you have 1 stitch left on each needle.

Insert your needle into the first stitch on the front needle as if to knit. Pull this stitch off the needle.

Insert your needle into the first stitch on the back needle as if to purl. Pull this stitch off the needle.

You may need to adjust the tension of the stitches on this row.

Starting on the right side of the row, pull up the right side of the stitch, then pull up the left. Continue across the row.

elle
mittens

ONE SIZE: To fit an average sized womans hand.

YARN USED: 2 x 100g balls of Rowan Cocoon (shown in shade Dove 849)

NEEDLES: 5mm double pointed needles

TENSION: 14sts and 22rows = 10cm measured over stocking stitch using 5mm needles.

EXTRAS: Stitch holder

Using 4x 5mm double-pointed needles, cast on 28sts and distribute as follows: 9sts on the first needle, 10sts on the second needle, and 9sts on the third needle. Join in round, and then proceed as follows:

Round 1: (K2, P2) to end.
Rep last round until work meas 16cm.

Knit 4 rounds.

THUMB GUSSET
Set-up Round 1: M1, knit to end.
Round 1: Knit
Round 2: K1, M1, knit to end, M1.
Rep last 2 rounds until there are 16sts on the first needle, ending after a round 1. 41sts

Next Round: Put first 7 stitches from the first needle and final 6 stitches from the third needle onto a stitch holder, to work later as thumb. 28sts

Continue in stocking stitch, beginning at the first stitch on needle 1, joining the sts back into a round. Knit until work meas 8cm from the thumb break.

SHAPE TOP OF MITTEN:
Round 1: *Sl1, K1, psso, K10, K2tog; rep from * once more. 24sts
Rounds 2-3: Knit.
Round 4: *Sl1, K1, psso, K8, K2tog; rep

from * once more. 20sts
Rounds 5-6: Knit.
Round 7: *Sl1, K1, psso, K6, K2tog;
rep from * once more. 16sts
Round 8: Knit.
Round 9: *Sl1, K1, psso, K4, K2tog;
rep from * once more. 12sts
Round 10: *Sl1, K1, psso, K2, K2tog;
rep from * once more. 8sts
Round 11: Sl1, K2tog, psso, rep from
* once more, K2. 4sts.

Cut yarn, thread through rem sts, and
pull tight.

THUMB
Slip the 13 thumb sts from stitch
holder onto needles as follows:
5sts on the first needle, 5 sts on the
second needle, and 3 sts on the third
needle.

Next Round: Knit, picking up 3 extra
sts from the gap above the gusset.
16 sts

Continue in stocking stitch until
thumb meas 6cm.

Next Round: K2tog to end. 8 sts

Cut yarn, thread through rem sts, and
pull tight.

izabel
wrap

YARN USAGE: 17 x 50g balls of Rowan Softyak DK (shown in Plain – 232)

NEEDLES: 4mm (6US) circular needles at least 80cm long

TENSION: 22sts and 30rows = 10cm measured over stocking stitch using 4mm needles

EXTRAS: Stitch holders

APPROX FINISHED MEASUREMENTS: 68cm x 134cm

Using 4mm needles, cast on 294sts.
Row 1: (RS) (K1, P1) to end.
Row 2: (P1, K1) to end.
Rep last 2 rows twice more.

Starting with a knit row, work 40 rows in stocking stitch.

Work in (K1, P1) moss stitch for 40 rows.

Rep last 80 rows once more, then 40 rows of stocking stitch once more

Next Row: Knit 147sts, turn. Place rem sts on stitch holder.

Working on live stitches for right front, work 80-row repeat until right front matches back, ending after the 6 rows of (K1, P1) moss stitch.

Cast off.

Return stitches on holder to needles and work left front as for right front.

FINISHING
Press as described on the information page.

heidi

scarf

YARN USAGE: Rowan Kidsilk Haze
A – Pearl 590 x 2 balls
B – Grace 580 x 2 balls
C – Shadow 653 x 2 balls
D – Majestic 589 x 2 balls
E – Cream 634 x 2 balls

NEEDLES: 5mm (8US)

TENSION: 16sts and 26rows = 10cm
measured over stocking stitch using
5mm needles and yarn held double

APPROX FINISHED MEASUREMENTS:
270cm x 22.5cm

Using 5mm needles and yarn A held
double, cast on 36sts.
Row 1: Knit.
Row 2: K4, purl to last 4sts, K4.
Rep last 2 rows throughout.

Continue until yarn A is used up, ending
after a WS row.
Change to yarn E, continue for 36cm,
ending after a WS row. Break off yarn E.
Change to yarn B, continue until all yarn
is used, ending after a WS row.
Change to yarn E, continue for 36cm,
ending after a WS row. Break off yarn E.
Change to yarn C, continue until all yarn
is used, ending after a WS row.
Change to yarn E, continue for 36cm,
ending after a WS row. Break off yarn E.
Change to yarn D, continue until all yarn
is used, ending after a WS row.

FINISHING
Press as described on the
information page.

Fold scarf in half length-ways, with
wrong sides together.

Using mattress stitch, join the side seams
together, and then the cast-on and cast-
off edges.

Abbreviations

K – knit

P – purl

st(s) – stitch(es)

inc – increas(e)(ing)

dec – decreas(e)(ing)

st st – stocking stitch (1 row knit, 1 row purl)

g st – garter stitch (every row knit)

beg – begin(ning)

foll – following

rem – remain(ing)

alt – alternate

cont – continue

patt – pattern

tog – together

mm – millimetres

cm – centimetres

in – inch(es)

RS – right side

WS – wrong side

sl 1 – slip one stitch

psso – pass slipped stitch over

tbl – through back of loop

m1 – make one stitch by picking up loop between last and next stitch and working into the back of this loop

yfwd - bring yarn forward between the needles and then back over before making the next stitch.

yrn – yarn round needle. Wrap yarn around the needle back to a purl position.

ROWAN STOCKISTS

AUSTRALIA: Australian Country Spinners, Pty Ltd, Level 7, 409 St. Kilda Road, Melbourne Vic 3004. Tel: 03 9380 3888 Fax: 03 9820 0989 Email: customerservice@auspinners.com.au

Morris and Sons 50 York Street, Sydney NSW 2000
Tel: 02 92998588

Morris and Sons Level 1, 234 Collins Street, Melbourne Vic 3000
Tel: 03 9654 0888

AUSTRIA: MEZ Harlander GmbH, Schulhof 6, 1. Stock, 1010 Wien, Austria Tel: + 00800 26 27 28 00 Fax: (00) 49 7644 802-133 Email: verkauf.harlander@mezcrafts.com

BELGIUM: MEZ crafts Belgium NV, c/o MEZ GmbH, Kaiserstr.1, 79341 Kenzingen Germany Tel: 0032 (0) 800 77 89 2 Fax: 00 49 7644 802 133 Email: sales.be-nl@mezcrafts.com

BULGARIA: MEZ Crafts Bulgaria EOOD, 7 Magnaurska Shkola Str., BG-1784 Sofia, Bulgaria Tel: (+359 2) 439 24 24 Fax: (+359 2) 976 77 20 Email: office.bg@mezcrafts.com

CANADA: Sirdar USA Inc. 406 20th Street SE, Hickory, North Carolina, USA 28602 Tel: 828 404 3705 Fax: 828 404 3707 Email: sirdarusa@sirdar.co.uk

CHINA: Commercial agent Mr Victor Li, c/o MEZ GmbH Germany, Kaiserstr. 1, 79341 Kenzingen / Germany Tel: (86- 21) 13816681825 Email: victor.li@mezcrafts.com

CHINA: Shanghai Yujun CO.LTD., Room 701 Wangjiao Plaza, No.175 Yan'an (E), 200002 Shanghai, China Tel: +86 2163739785 Email: jessechang@vip.163.com

CYPRUS: MEZ Crafts Bulgaria EOOD, 7 Magnaurska Shkola Str., BG-1784 Sofia, Bulgaria Tel: (+359 2) 439 34 24 Fax: (+359 2) 976 77 20 Email: marketing.cy@mezcrafts.com

CZECH REPUBLIC: Coats Czecho s.r.o.Staré Mesto 246 569 32 Tel: (420) 461616633 Email: galanterie@coats.com

DENMARK: Carl J. Permin A/S Egegaardsvej 28 DK-2610 Rødovre Tel: (45) 36 36 89 89 Email: permin@permin.dk

ESTONIA: MEZ Crafts Estonia OÜ, Ampri tee 9/4, 74001 Viimsi Harjumaa Tel: +372 630 6252 Email: info.ee@mezcrafts.com

FINLAND: Prym Consumer Finland Oy, Huhtimontie 6, 04200 KERAVA Tel: +358 9 274871

FRANCE: 3bcom, 35 avenue de Larrieu, 31094 Toulouse cedex 01, France
Tel: 0033 (0) 562 202 096 Email: Commercial@3b-com.com

GERMANY: MEZ GmbH, Kaiserstr. 1, 79341 Kenzingen, Germany Tel: 0049 7644 802 222 Email: kenzingen.vertrieb@mezcrafts.com Fax: 0049 7644 802 300

GREECE: MEZ Crafts Bulgaria EOOD, 7 Magnaurska Shkola Str., BG-1784 Sofia, Bulgaria Tel: (+359 2) 439 24 24 Fax: (+359 2) 976 77 20 Email: office.bg@mezcrafts.com

HOLLAND: G. Brouwer & Zn B.V., Oudhuijzerweg 69, 3648 AB Wilnis Tel: 0031 (0) 297-281 557 Email: info@gbrouwer.nl

HONG KONG: East Unity Company Ltd, Unit B2, 7/F., Block B, Kailey Industrial Centre, 12 Fung Yip Street, Chai Wan Tel: (852)2869 7110 Email: eastunityco@yahoo.com.hk

ICELAND: Carl J. Permin A/S Egegaardsvej 28, DK-2610 Rødovre Tel: (45) 36 36 89 89 Email: permin@permin.dk

ITALY: Mez Cucirini Italy Srl, Viale Sarca, 223, 20126 MILANO Tel: 0039 0264109080 Email: servizio.clienti@mezcrafts.com Fax: 02 64109080

JAPAN: Hobbyra Hobbyre Corporation, 23-37, 5-Chome, Higashi-Ohi, Shinagawa-Ku, 1400011 Tokyo. Tel: +81334721104 Daidoh International, 3-8-11 Kudanminami Chiyodaku, Hiei Kudan Bldg 5F, 1018619 Tokyo. Tel +81-3-3222-7076, Fax +81-3-3222-7066

KOREA: My Knit Studio, 3F, 144 Gwanhun-Dong, 110-300 Jongno-Gu, Seoul Tel: 82-2-722-0006 Email: myknit@myknit.com

LATVIA: Latvian Crafts, 12-2, Jurġu street, LV-2011 Tel: +371 37 126326825 Email: vjelkins@latviancrafts.lv

LEBANON: y.knot, Saifi Village, Mkhalissiya Street 162, Beirut Tel: (961) 1 992211 Fax: (961) 1 315553 Email: y.knot@cyberia.net.lb

LITHUANIA: MEZ Crafts Lithuania UAB, A. Juozapavicious str. 6/2, LT-09310 Vilnius Tel: +370 527 30971 Fax: +370 527 2305 Email: info.lt@mezcrafts.com

LUXEMBOURG: MEZ GmbH, Kaiserstr.1, 79341 Kenzingen, Germany Tel: 00 49 7644 802 222 Email: kenzingen.vertrieb@mezcrafts.com

MEXICO: Estambres Crochet SA de CV, Aaron Saenz 1891-7Pte, 64650 MONTERREY
TEL +52 (81) 8335-3870 Email: abremer@redmundial.com.mx

NEW ZEALAND: ACS New Zealand, P.O Box 76199, Northwood, Christchurch, New Zealand Tel: 64 3 323 6665 Fax: 64 3 323 6660 Email: lynn@impactmg.co.nz

NORWAY: Carl J. Permin A/S Egegaardsvej 28 DK-2610 Rødovre Tel: (45) 36 36 89 89 E-mail: permin@permin.dk

PORTUGAL: Mez Crafts Portugal, Lda – Av. Vasco da Gama, 774 - 4431-059 V.N, Gaia, Portugal Tel: 00 351 223 770700 Email: sales.iberia@mezcrafts.com

RUSSIA: Family Hobby, 124683, Moskau, Zelenograd, Haus 1505, Raum III Tel.: 007 (499) 270-32-47 Handtel. 007 916 213 74 04 Email: tv@fhobby.ruWeb: www.family-hobby.ru

SINGAPORE: Golden Dragon Store, 101 Upper Cross St. #02-51, People's Park Centre Tel: (65) 65358454 /65358234 Email: gdscraft@hotmail.com

SLOVAKIA: MEZ Crafts Slovakia, s.r.o. Seberiniho 1, 821 03 Bratislava, Slovakia Tel: +421 2 32 30 31 19 Email: galanteria@mezcrafts.com

SOUTH AFRICA: Arthur Bales LTD, 62 4th Avenue, Linden 2195 Tel: (27) 11 888 2401 Fax: (27) 11 782 6137 Email: arthurb@new.co.za

SPAIN: MEZ Fabra Spain S.A, Avda Meridiana 350, pta 13 D, 08027 Barcelona Tel: +34 932908400 Fax: +34 932908409 Email: atencion.clientes@mezcrafts.com

SWEDEN: Carl J. Permin A/S Egegaardsvej 28 DK-2610 Rødovre Tel: (45) 36 36 89 89 E-mail: permin@permin.dk

SWITZERLAND: MEZ Crafts Switzerland GmbH, c/o Puplicitas AG, Mürtenstrasse 39, 8048, Zürich Switzerland www.mezcrafts.com

TURKEY: MEZ Crafts Tekstil A.S, Kavacık Mahallesi, Ekinciler Cad. Necip Fazıl Sok. No.8 Kat: 5, 34810 Beykoz / Istanbul Tel: +90 216 425 88 10

TAIWAN: Cactus Quality Co Ltd, 7FL-2, No. 140, Sec.2 Roosevelt Rd, Taipei, 10084 Taiwan, R.O.C. Tel: 00886-2-23656527 Fax: 886-2-23656503 Email: cqcl@ms17.hinet.net

THAILAND: Global Wide Trading, 10 Lad Prao Soi 88, Bangkok 10310 Tel: 00 662 933 9019 Fax: 00 662 933 9110 Email: global.wide@yahoo.com

U.S.A.: Sirdar USA Inc. 406 20th Street SE, Hickory, North Carolina, USA 28602 Tel: 828 404 3705 Fax: 828 404 3707 Email: sirdarusa@sirdar.co.uk

U.K: Mez Crafts U.K, 17F Brooke's Mill, Armitage Bridge, Huddersfield, HD4 7NR Web: www.mezcrafts.com Tel: 01484 950630

Information

TENSION

This is the size of your knitting. Most of the knitting patterns will have a tension quoted. This is how many stitches 10cm/4in in width and how many rows 10cm/4in in length to make a square. If your knitting doesn't match this then your finished garment will not measure the correct size. To obtain the correct measurements for your garment you must achieve the tension.

The tension quoted on a ball band is the manufacturer's average. For the manufacturer and designers to produce designs they have to use a tension for you to be able to obtain the measurements quoted. It's fine not to be the average, but you need to know if you meet the average or not. Then you can make the necessary adjustments to obtain the correct measurements.

YARN

Keep one ball band from each project so that you have a record of what you have used and most importantly how to care for your garment after it has been completed. Always remember to give the ball band with the garment if it is a gift.

The ball band normally provides you with the average tension and recommended needle sizes for the yarn, this may vary from what has been used in the pattern, always go with the pattern as the designer may change needles to obtain a certain look. The ball band also tells you the name of the yarn and what it is made of, the weight and approximate length of the ball of yarn along with the shade and dye lot numbers. This is important as dye lots can vary, you need to buy your yarn with matching dye lots.

PRESSING AND AFTERCARE

Having spent so long knitting your project it can be a great shame not to look after it properly. Some yarns are suitable for pressing once you have finished to improve the look of the fabric. To find out this information you will need to look on the yarn ball band, where there will be washing and care symbols.

Once you have checked to see if your yarn is suitable to be pressed and the knitting is a smooth texture (stocking stitch for example), pin out and place a damp cloth onto the knitted pieces. Hold the steam iron (at the correct temperature) approximately 10cm/4in away from the fabric and steam. Keep the knitted pieces pinned in place until cool.

As a test it is a good idea to wash your tension square in the way you would expect to wash your garment.

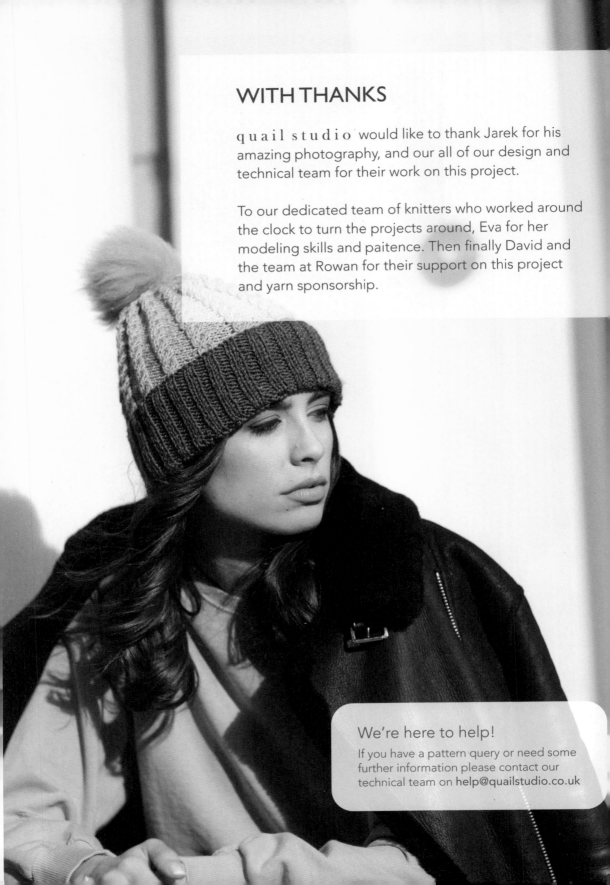

WITH THANKS

q u a i l s t u d i o would like to thank Jarek for his amazing photography, and our all of our design and technical team for their work on this project.

To our dedicated team of knitters who worked around the clock to turn the projects around, Eva for her modeling skills and paitence. Then finally David and the team at Rowan for their support on this project and yarn sponsorship.

We're here to help!

If you have a pattern query or need some further information please contact our technical team on help@quailstudio.co.uk